The Rat

by **Carolyn Sloan**
illustrated by **Michael Reid**

Hope wanted to help her dad. His car would not start. It would not go.

Hope saw a rat. The rat ran away and her dad didn't see it. But the boys did!

The boys ran after the rat but Hope hid it. She wanted to look after it.

The boys went away and the rat was safe.
It looked up at Hope.

The rat was a tame one. Hope took it to the hut. She said it would be safe there.

Hope called the rat Fred. She played with him. He was very tame and he liked playing with her.

Hope had to go home. She was going to get some food.

Beth and Scruff came to the hut.

Scruff came in and saw Fred. Beth saw him too. Fred ran away and hid from Scruff.

Ranjit and Kamal came in.

"Scruff saw a rat!" said Beth.

"Oh no!" said Ranjit.

Ranjit told his mum about the rat.

"Rats are pests," said Mum. "You must not go to that hut."

Mum told the pest man about the rat. She told him there were rats in the hut.

The pest man came to the hut. He put down some rat traps. He shut up the hut.

Hope came to the hut. Kamal told her about the pest man.

"He can't kill the rat!" shouted Hope.

"You can't kill rats," Hope said to the pest man. "Please, please don't do that!"

"Rats are pests," said the pest man. "You can't play in the hut if there are rats."

“What is it, Hope?” said Kamal. “Tell us.”

Hope told them it was *her* rat in the hut. She said Fred was a tame rat and he was her pet.

The pest man let Hope go in the hut.
Hope came out with Fred.

The man went off.

"You can keep your hut," he said, "but keep your rat at home!"

Hope went home to see her mum and dad.
Dad looked at the rat. He liked him.

"Can I have him?" said Hope.

"Will you look after him?" said Mum.

"Yes," said Hope

"OK," said Mum. "You can keep him."

So Fred came to live at Hope's house. She had a new pet and Fred had a new home.